# Home
## IS WHERE
## THE
# Kitchen Is

### DELICIOUS RECIPES FROM MY KITCHEN TO YOURS

## ALICIA M. CURRY

HOME IS WHERE THE KITCHEN IS
*Delicious Recipes from My Kitchen to Yours*

iUniverse books may be ordered through booksellers or by contacting:

iUniverse
1663 Liberty Drive
Bloomington, IN 47403
www.iuniverse.com
844-349-9409

ISBN: 978-1-6632-6031-4 (sc)
ISBN: 978-1-6632-5994-3 (hc)
ISBN: 978-1-6632-5995-0 (e)

Library of Congress Control Number: 2024902684

Print information available on the last page.

iUniverse rev. date: 04/15/2024

This book is dedicated first to God, and then to my wonderful family and friends, who love my food and believed I could do this.

I love you guys.

# CONTENTS

Baked Chicken

# Baked Chicken

Prep time: 20 minutes. Cook time: 3 hours. Serves 4–6.

12 whole chicken wings
1 tablespoon onion powder
1 tablespoon garlic powder
1 tablespoon paprika
1 tablespoon black pepper
1 teaspoon cayenne pepper
1 stick unsalted butter, sliced
1 large onion, diced
2 bell peppers, diced
2 teaspoons minced garlic
1/3 cup low-sodium chicken broth
1 (8-ounce) can cream of mushroom
1 (8-ounce) can cream of chicken
1 (8-ounce) can cream of celery

Preheat oven to 350 degrees F. Place chicken wings in a baking dish. Shake each seasoning evenly over each chicken wing: onion powder garlic powder, paprika, black pepper, and cayenne pepper. Add pats of butter evenly on top of each wing.

Dice onion and bell peppers and mix with minced garlic in a small bowl. Spread vegetable mixture evenly on top of chicken.

Pour chicken broth, cream of mushroom, cream of chicken, and cream of celery evenly into dish.

Cover dish and place in oven for 2 hours. Then, uncover and bake uncovered for 1 additional hour.

Enjoy!

ALICIA M. CURRY

Fried
Pork Ribs

# Fried Pork Ribs

Prep time: 20 minutes. Serves 4–6.

1 full slab pork ribs, sliced
1 tablespoon sea salt
1 tablespoon black pepper
1 tablespoon paprika
1 tablespoon brown sugar
4–8 cups of corn oil
2 teaspoons unsalted butter

Slice slab into individual ribs and season with salt, pepper, paprika, and brown sugar.

In a frying pan on medium-high heat, add corn oil and butter.

Once oil is heated, use tongs to slowly add seasoned ribs to the pan. Fry a few pieces at a time. Flip every 5–7 minutes until golden brown.

Place fried ribs on paper towels to drain grease off before plating.

Add desired sauce and enjoy!

ALICIA M. CURRY

Red
Beans
and Rice

# Red Beans and Rice

Prep time: 15 minutes. Cook time: 2 1/2 to 3 hours. Serves 6—8.

1 (16-ounce) bag red kidney beans
3 (32-ounce) boxes low-sodium chicken broth
2 cups water
1 large onion, diced
1 bell pepper, diced
2 stalks celery, diced
1 bunch green onion, diced
1 teaspoon minced garlic
1 teaspoon liquid crawfish boil
2 sticks unsalted butter
1 teaspoon cayenne pepper
1/4 cup Cajun seasoning
3 bay leaves
16 ounces smoked sausage
6—8 servings cooked rice

In a large pot, add beans, 2 boxes of chicken broth, and water. For slow cooking, set to low-medium heat.

Dice onion, bell pepper, celery, and green onion.

Add diced vegetables, minced garlic, and crawfish boil to pot. Season with cayenne pepper and Cajun seasoning. Add 1 stick of butter and bring to a boil. Stir pot to mix all ingredients well.

Add the last box of broth and cook for 1 hour, stirring every 20 minutes. Add more water as needed.

Add second stick of butter, lightly smashing beans until mixture is a gravy-like consistency. Continue to stir periodically for about an hour, or until beans are tender, adding water as needed.

Remove from heat. Serve over rice.

*Shrimp*
*Fried Rice*

# Shrimp Fried Rice

Prep time: 20 minutes. Cook time: 35 minutes. Serves 4–6.

16 ounces jumbo shrimp
1 bunch green onions, diced
1/4 cup sesame oil
1 teaspoon unsalted butter
2 eggs
1/2 cup soy sauce
4–6 servings cooked rice
1/3 cup frozen peas
1/3 cup frozen carrots

Dice green onions and set aside.
In skillet, heat and coat with sesame oil over medium-high heat. Add shrimp and cook until pink is gone. While shrimp cooks, cook eggs in a separate pan.
In a small frying pan, heat 1 teaspoon butter. Add 2 eggs and scramble until yolks are no longer runny. Set scrambled eggs aside.
Once eggs are cooked in frying pan, shrimp in skillet should be done. When done, remove shrimp from skillet and set it aside.
In skillet, add sesame oil and soy sauce. Add cooked rice to coated skillet. Add additional soy sauce as needed to brown the rice. Once rice is browned, add thawed peas and carrots, and add the scrambled eggs that were set aside. Stir continuously.
Once mixed, add shrimp and green onion. Stir for 5 minutes.
Remove from heat, plate, and enjoy!

ALICIA M. CURRY

Stuffed
Bell Peppers

# Stuffed Bell Peppers

Prep time: 45 minutes. Cook time: 2 hours. Serves 8.

4 bell peppers, halved
1 bell pepper, diced
1 large onion, diced
1 pound smoked sausage, diced
1 box cornbread mix
1 pound ground turkey
1/4 cup Cajun seasoning
1/4 cup onion powder
1/4 cup garlic power
1 teaspoon cayenne pepper
1/4 cup minced garlic
1 package imitation crab meat
1 pound popcorn shrimp
2 cups low-sodium chicken broth
1 cup breadcrumbs

Preheat oven to 375 degrees F.
In a large pot, fill halfway with water and boil.
Add halve 4 bell peppers and add halved bell peppers to boiling water. Boil halved bell peppers for 15 minutes.
While peppers boil, dice 1 additional bell pepper, onion, and smoked sausage and set aside.
Prepare cornbread mix and bake according to box instructions.
In a large skillet, brown ground turkey. Add Cajun seasoning, onion powder, garlic powder, and cayenne pepper.
Once browned and seasoned, add diced bell pepper, onion, minced garlic, and smoked sausage to skillet. Add imitation crabmeat and cook for 10 minutes. Add shrimp and cook until shrimp is no longer pink.
Remove halved peppers from heat, and drain pot. Arrange peppers like cups on a large, greased baking sheet.
Remove cornbread from oven.
In a large mixing bowl, add cornbread and meat mixture from skillet. Add 1 cup chicken broth. Mix well.
Add 1/2 cup breadcrumbs and additional 1 cup chicken broth. Mix well. Mixture should be a stuffing consistency.
Spoon mixture into halved peppers until full. Sprinkle remaining breadcrumbs on top of each pepper.
Bake stuffed peppers for 20–25 minutes until browned.
Remove from oven, let cool, and enjoy!

ALICIA M. CURRY

# Baked Macaroni and Shrimp Casserole

# Baked Macaroni and Shrimp Casserole

Prep time: 35 minutes. Cook time: 1 hour. Serves 6–10.

1 pound elbow pasta
1 stick butter
1 onion, diced
1 bell pepper, diced
1 scallion, diced
1 pound shrimp
1/4 cup Cajun seasoning
1/3 cup shredded Gouda cheese
1/3 cup shredded Havarti cheese
1/3 cup shredded cheddar cheese
1/3 cup shredded pepper jack cheese
1/2 cup sour cream
1 (8-ounce) can evaporated milk
1 cup buttermilk
1/2 cup milk

Preheat oven to 350 degrees F.
In medium saucepan, heat water to boil.
Dice onions, bell pepper, and scallions.
In skillet, melt 1 teaspoon butter. Add diced onions, bell pepper, scallions, and shrimp, and sauté.
Add pasta to boiling water and cook until al dente. Drain cooked pasta.
In mixing bowl, add pasta, Cajun seasoning, Gouda, Havarti, cheddar, pepper jack, sour cream, milk, evaporated milk, buttermilk, and shrimp mixture. Mix well until all blended and creamy.
In greased casserole dish, add mixture and top with additional cheese.
Bake until golden brown. Remove from heat, cool, plate, and enjoy!

ALICIA M. CURRY

*Fried Potatoes with Onions*

# Fried Potatoes with Onions

Prep time: 15 minutes. Cook time: 35 minutes. Serves 6-8.

8 russet potatoes, quartered
1 large onion, diced
1/4 cup olive oil
2 tablespoon garlic salt
1 tablespoon black pepper
1 stick unsalted butter

Rinse potatoes, pat dry, and cut into pieces. In a mixing bowl, add potatoes, olive oil, garlic salt, and black pepper. Dice onion.
In a skillet, melt half stick butter over medium-high heat. Add seasoned potatoes and onion. Stir consistently until potatoes are tender and golden brown.
Add remaining half stick butter and stir until caramelized.
Remove from heat, plate, and enjoy!

ALICIA M. CURRY

*Pepperoni Pizza Dip*

# Pepperoni Pizza Dip

Prep time: 15 minutes. Cook time: 20 minutes. Serves 3–4.

1 (16-ounce) jar pizza sauce
1 teaspoon garlic salt
1 teaspoon black pepper
12–14 pieces sliced pepperoni
1/2 cup of Italian blend cheese
1/2 cup mozzarella cheese
1 teaspoon parsley flakes
8 slices garlic bread

Preheat oven to 400 degrees F.
In a cast-iron skillet, add pizza sauce, salt and pepper. Stir well.
Fold pepperoni slices into sauce.
Top with Italian and mozzarella cheese, and sprinkle parsley flakes on top.
Bake until cheese is browned.
Bake garlic bread according to box instructions.
Remove from oven, cool, dip, and enjoy!

ALICIA M. CURRY

# Shrimp and Chicken Alfredo with Spinach

# Shrimp and Chicken Alfredo with Spinach

Prep time: 20 minutes. Cook time: 1 hour. Serves 6–8.

1 onion, diced
1 bell pepper, diced
1 pound shrimp
2 sticks unsalted butter
1 pound fettuccine
1 teaspoon sea salt
1 teaspoon black pepper
1 teaspoon cayenne pepper
1 tablespoon Cajun seasoning
1 cup buttermilk
1/2 cup parmesan cheese
1 pound chicken tenderloin (diced)
2 (16-ounce) jars alfredo sauce
1 bag baby spinach

## Garnish
1 tablespoon parsley flakes

In a large pot, heat water to boil.
Dice onion and bell pepper.
In a saucepan, add half stick of butter, shrimp, diced onions, and bell pepper. Sauté.
Add fettuccine to large pot and boil until al dente.
To saucepan, add sea salt, black pepper, cayenne pepper, Cajun seasoning, 1 stick of butter, buttermilk, and parmesan cheese. Heat to simmer.
Add 2 jars of alfredo sauce to saucepan and stir periodically until it simmers.
Add half bag of spinach, stirring until tender. Add remaining spinach. Simmer 10 minutes, stirring periodically.
Remove from heat.
Garnish with parsley flakes, plate and enjoy!

ALICIA M. CURRY

# Collards, Cabbage, and Corn with Smoked Meat

# Collards, Cabbage, and Corn with Smoked Meat

Prep time: 30 minutes. Cook time: 2 hours. Serves 8–10.

1 bunch collards, chopped
1 head cabbage, chopped
1 cup white distilled vinegar
3 turkey tails
1/2 stick unsalted butter
1 large onion, diced
1/2 cup greens seasoning
2 bay leaves
4 (32-ounce) chicken broth
6 ears corn

Chop cabbage and collards. In separate mixing bowls, soak in water with white vinegar to clean.
In small pot, boil turkey tails until tender. Drain water. Add 1/2 stick butter and heat to simmer.
Dice large onion.
To pot, add diced onion, greens seasoning, and bay leaves. Simmer 10 minutes.
Drain collards and cabbage, and rinse.
To pot, add 2 boxes chicken broth and collards. Cook for 1 hour or until tender.
Add cabbage to pot and cook down, stirring periodically for 30 minutes.
Add turkey tails and corn, stirring periodically an additional 30 minutes. Turkey
Tail meat should fall off the bone, making it easier to mix.
Remove from heat and cover.
Plate when ready and enjoy!

ALICIA M. CURRY

Jambalaya
Pasta

# Jambalaya Pasta

Prep time: 15 minutes. Cook time: 1 hour. Serves 6–8.

1 pound smoked sausage, diced
1 pound chicken tenderloin, diced
1 pound medium shrimp
1 onion, diced
1 bell pepper, diced
1 teaspoon garlic powder
1 teaspoon onion powder
1 teaspoon white pepper
1/2 stick unsalted butter
1/4 cup minced garlic
2 (16-ounce) jars traditional red sauce
1 tablespoon sugar
1/4 cup gumbo seasoning
2 tablespoon cayenne pepper
5 bay leaves
1/4 cup Cajun seasoning
1 pound rotini pasta

**Garnish**
1/4 cup parsley

Dice sausage, chicken, onion, and bell pepper.
In separate containers, season sausage, chicken, and shrimp each with garlic powder, onion powder, and white pepper. Set aside.
In medium saucepan, heat half stick butter on medium-high heat to simmer. Add minced garlic, onion, and bell pepper. Simmer until tender.
Add chicken and cook until brown.
Add smoked sausage. Cook for ten minutes.
Add shrimp and cook until pink.
Add two jars of red sauce, sugar, gumbo seasoning, cayenne pepper, bay leaves, and
Cajun seasoning. Cover for 25 minutes and simmer on low.
In a pot, heat water to boil. Add rotini pasta and cook to al dente.
Add pasta to sauce and mix.
Pour into a dish and garnish with parsley.
Plate and enjoy!

ALICIA M. CURRY

*Enchiladas*

# Enchiladas

Prep time: 15 minutes. Cook time: 40 minutes. Serves 4–6.

1 pound ground turkey, beef, chicken, or shrimp
1/2 poblano pepper, diced
1/2 onion, diced
1/2 cup taco seasoning
1 cup water
10 flour tortillas
1 (16-ounce) jar taco sauce
1 (8-ounce) shredded queso cheese

## Serve With
1 (8-ounce) bag shredded lettuce
4 ounces jalapeno peppers
2 Roma tomatoes, diced
Catalina dressing to taste

Preheat oven to 375 degrees F.
Dice Roma tomatoes and set aside. Dice poblano and onion.
In medium pan, heat chosen meat to temperature.
Add poblano and onion and cook until tender.
Add taco seasoning and water. Mix well.
Spoon 2 tablespoons of meat mixture into each tortilla. Roll filled tortilla.
In casserole dish or baking sheet, add filled tortillas in a row. Top with taco sauce and shredded cheese.
Bake 25 minutes or until cheese is melted and browned.
Remove from oven. Serve with shredded lettuce, jalapeno peppers, tomatoes, and Catalina dressing.
Enjoy!

ALICIA M. CURRY

Shrimp
Po' Boys

# Shrimp Po' Boys

Prep time: 15 minutes. Cook time: 10 minutes. Serves 3-4.

2 pounds jumbo shrimp
1 teaspoon Ole Bay seasoning
1 teaspoon white pepper
1 teaspoon Cajun seasoning
corn oil
1 package shrimp fry
1 loaf French bread, halved
1 tomato, sliced
1 jar hamburger dill pickles
1 (8-ounce) bag shredded lettuce

## Dressing
1/4 cup mayonnaise
1/4 cup ketchup
2 tablespoons hot sauce

In large frying pan on medium-high heat, add corn oil.
Devein and season shrimp with Ole Bay, white pepper, and Cajun seasoning.
In a bowl, add shrimp fry and seasoned shrimp. Set aside until oil is hot.
Once oil is heated, use tongs to slowly add seasoned shrimp to the pan. Fry a few pieces at a time.
Flip every 5 minutes.
Place fried shrimp on paper towels to drain grease off before plating.
Slice French bread in half horizontally to make a sandwich.
Mix mayonnaise, ketchup, and hot sauce. Spread sauce on both sides of bread.
Add shrimp to bottom half of sandwich. Add lettuce, pickles, and tomato as desired, and put top of French bread on top. Cut into 3-4 sandwiches, plate, and enjoy!

Cucumber
Salad

# Cucumber Salad

Prep time: 20 minutes. Serves 6–10.

2 cucumbers, sliced and halved
1 large red onion, sliced
3 Roma tomatoes, diced
strawberries, sliced
Italian dressing to taste
raspberry vinaigrette to taste
1 teaspoon sea salt
1 tablespoon black pepper

Chop cucumber, onion, tomatoes, and strawberries.
In bowl with lid, add chopped vegetables and fruit, Italian dressing, raspberry vinaigrette, salt, and pepper.
Close lid and shake well. Refrigerate for 30 minutes.
Enjoy!

ALICIA M. CURRY

*Summertime Salad*

# Summertime Salad

Prep time: 25 minutes. Serves 10–15.

1 head romaine lettuce, chopped
1 red onion, sliced
1 cucumber, diced
1 cup fresh strawberries, sliced
6 hard-boiled eggs, sliced
3 Roma tomatoes, sliced
1 (8-ounce) bag baby spinach
2 ounces salad topping
1 cup fresh blueberries

**Garnish**
parmesan cheese to taste
croutons as desired
salad dressing as desired

Chop romaine lettuce, onion, cucumber, strawberries, eggs, and tomatoes.
In a large bowl, add lettuce, onion, cucumber, spinach, and tomatoes. Top with salad topping, egg slices, strawberries, and blueberries.
Chill in the refrigerator for 1 hour.
Garnish with cheese, croutons, and dressing as desired and enjoy!

ALICIA M. CURRY

# Collard Greens with Smoked Meat

# Collard Greens with Smoked Meat

Prep time: 20 minutes. Cook time: 3 hours. Serves 4–8.

1 1/2 large onion, sliced
1 stick unsalted butter
2 bunches collards, chopped
1 cup vinegar
4 (32-ounce) boxes low-sodium chicken broth
3 turkey tails
8 ounces greens seasoning
1 teaspoon crushed red pepper flakes
1 teaspoon sugar

Slice onion.
In large pot, heat butter until simmer. Add onions.
Chop collards. Soak in water and vinegar to clean.
To large pot, add 2 boxes chicken broth and bring to a boil.
Add greens seasoning and turkey tails. Cover and simmer for 2 hours.
Add 2 additional boxes of chicken broth and crushed peppers to pot. Cover and cook on low heat for 1 hr.
Remove from heat, plate, and enjoy!

ALICIA M. CURRY

*Chili Mac*

# Chili Mac

Prep time: 25 minutes. Cook time: 45 minutes to 1 hour. Serves 4-6.

1 pound ground turkey
1 pound elbow pasta
1 onion, diced
1 bell pepper, diced
2 tablespoon minced garlic
1/4 cup chili powder
1 teaspoon garlic powder
1 teaspoon onion powder
1 tablespoon Italian seasoning
2 (16-ounce) jars traditional red sauce
2 tablespoon sugar

In a large pot, heat water to boil. When ready, add elbow pasta and cook to al dente.
Dice onion and bell pepper.
In a skillet, add turkey, onion, bell pepper, minced garlic, chili powder, onion powder, Italian seasoning, and sugar.
Drain excess oil. Add red sauce. Stir well and return to simmer.
Add pasta to chili and remove from heat.
Plate and enjoy!

ALICIA M. CURRY

Fried
Salmon

# Fried Salmon

Prep time: 25 minutes. Cook time: 30 minutes. Serves 4–6.

6 salmon steaks
1 lemon, halved
32 ounces corn oil
1/4 cup olive oil
1 tablespoon Cajun seasoning
1 tablespoon white pepper
seafood fry
3 tablespoon unsalted butter

**Garnish**
parsley flakes

In cast-iron skillet, heat corn oil on medium-high.
Halve lemon.
In a bowl, add salmon steaks and squeeze lemon juice over steaks. Add Cajun seasoning and white pepper. Drench in seafood fry.
Once oil is heated, use tongs to slowly add seasoned salmon to the pan. Fry two pieces at a time. Flip every 10 minutes or until golden brown.
Place salmon on paper towels to drain grease off before plating.
Sprinkle with parsley, plate, and enjoy!

ALICIA M. CURRY

*Succulent Kale*

# Succulent Kale

Prep time: 15 minutes. Cook time: 40 minutes. Serves 4–8.

2 bunches kale, chopped
1 cup white vinegar
1/4 cup coconut oil
1 bell pepper, diced
1 red onion, diced
1 bunch green onion, diced
2 tablespoon minced garlic
1 (8-ounce) can chicken broth

Chop kale. Soak in water and vinegar to clean.

In a medium cast-iron skillet, heat coconut oil over medium-high heat.

Dice bell peppers, onion, and green onion. Add diced vegetables and minced garlic to skillet and simmer.

Drain and rinse kale. Add kale to skillet. Gently fold and mix with vegetables. Let fry in pan until kale is soft and tender.

Add can of chicken broth to pan and simmer for 15 to 20 minutes.

Remove from heat, plate, and enjoy!

ALICIA M. CURRY

Tuscan
Shrimp
Pasta

# Tuscan Shrimp Pasta

Prep time: 15 minutes.
Cook time: 45 minutes.
Serves 4-6 people

1 pound fettuccine pasta
2 pounds jumbo shrimp
1 tablespoon sea salt
2 tablespoon white or black pepper
1 tablespoon Cajun seasoning
2 tablespoon olive oil
4 teaspoons unsalted butter
1 1/2 cups cherry tomatoes, halved
1/4 cup minced garlic
1/2-1 cup buttermilk
1 tablespoon oregano
3 ounces baby spinach
1/4 cup parmesan cheese

In a large pot, heat water to boil. When ready, add fettucine and cook to al dente.
In a bowl, add sea salt, pepper, and Cajun seasoning to shrimp and mix well.
In a skillet, warm olive oil and 2 teaspoons butter.
Once oil is heated, add shrimp to skillet and cook until pink. Flip periodically.
Place fried shrimp on paper towels and set aside.
To skillet, add tomatoes and minced garlic. Sauté for 5 minutes or until soft.
Add buttermilk and oregano and heat to boiling.
Return shrimp to skillet. Add baby spinach and cook until spinach is tender.
Remove from heat and add parmesan cheese. Plate and enjoy!

ALICIA M. CURRY

Gourmet
Pork and
Beans

# Gourmet Pork and Beans

Prep time: xx. Cook time: 35 minutes. Serves 4-6.

1 pack franks, sliced
1 (48-ounce) can pork and beans
1 stick unsalted butter
1 onion, diced
1/4 brown sugar
4 tablespoon white sugar
4 teaspoon black pepper
4 teaspoon sea salt

Slice franks.
In a medium pot, add all ingredients and warm over medium-high heat. Heat to boiling. Once boiling, reduce to medium-low heat until franks enlarge.
Remove from heat and cover until ready to bowl. Enjoy!

ALICIA M. CURRY

*Dirty Rice*

# Dirty Rice

Prep time: 5 minutes. Cook time: 45 minutes. Serves 4-6.

3 cups long grain rice, cleaned
2 pounds ground turkey or beef
1 large onion, diced
2 bell peppers, diced
1/4 cup minced garlic
1/4 Cajun seasoning
2 tablespoon garlic salt
2 tablespoon onion powder
1 teaspoon cayenne pepper
1/2 stick unsalted butter

**Garnish**
2 teaspoon parsley flakes

Preheat oven to 350 degrees F.
In a medium saucepan, cook rice according to bag instructions.
In a skillet, add ground meat and cook until browned.
Dice onion and bell peppers.
Add onions, bell peppers, and minced garlic to skillet. Simmer until veggies are tender.
Add Cajun seasoning, garlic salt, onion powder, cayenne pepper, and butter to skillet. Heat until butter is melted. Stir periodically.
Add cooked rice to skillet and mix well. Spoon rice mixture into casserole dish.
Cover with foil and bake for 15 minutes.
Remove from oven, garnish with parsley, plate, and enjoy!

Printed in the United States
by Baker & Taylor Publisher Services